45 creative homily resources for children
from pre-school through third grade arranged
by seasons and themes.

GOD'S WORD FOR Little ONES

Anne Hirsch Shaughnessy

AVE MARIA PRESS   Notre Dame, Indiana 46556

International Standard Book Number: 0-87793-464-9

Library of Congress Catalog Card Number: 91-72860

Book design and text illustrations by Elizabeth J. French
Cover and chapter opener art by Sarah Geissler Smiley

Printed and bound in the United States of America.

Contents

Introduction

To capture and hold the attention of children while trying to help them understand and think more deeply about our faith can sound impossible. But it's not! Bringing scripture to life for children can be fun, exciting, and challenging.

This book contains the resources for forty-five children's homilies that are ideal for use with children's liturgies — especially liturgy of the word programs. Teachers and catechists will also find them useful in various religious education classes and projects such as illustrating a parable or a lesson from scripture.

Most include a suggested scripture reading; each one also includes preparation and props needed for the presentation, and a short homily (or lesson) designed to relate the scripture reading or theme to something the children can understand and apply to their lives.

The first four sections of the book are arranged around the liturgical season. Many of the homily/lesson ideas are based on Sunday scripture readings, which makes them particularly useful in preparing for or celebrating the Sunday liturgy with children. The index at the end of the book can serve as a quick reference to the scripture passages used for the homilies.

Part Four, "Being the People of God," contains theme celebrations for Christian community, following Jesus, and the sacraments of baptism, eucharist, and reconciliation. Part Six covers celebrations that take place during the school year — Columbus Day, Thanksgiving Day, Valentine's Day, Mardi Gras, and the opening and closing of the school year.

These homilies/lessons will work particularly well with younger children (pre-school through third grade), but older children can learn from them as well. You may have to adapt them somewhat to suit the needs of your own group.

Here are a few practical tips for preparing and giving children's homilies:

— Use a children's lectionary or adapt the readings to the children's level. They can't make a connection with a reading if they don't understand the words.

— Ask questions about the readings instead of telling what the reading was about. The children learn quickly to listen to the readings so they can answer the questions. Repeat their answers for all to hear.

— Posters often arouse the children's curiosity about what is to come and remind them of the message throughout the rest of the liturgy or lesson. A roll of butcher paper and some tempera paint will make a lot of posters. Hang the posters in a prominent place and at the children's eye level. Be sure visuals are large enough for all to see and read. Read them aloud for the children who cannot read them.

Remember that children's activities take time to prepare. You will need to assemble any props you're going to use and allow time to set them up before the children arrive. Take time to read the scripture passage, prepare the homily/lesson, and adapt it to your own personality, situation, and group if necessary. I always find that this time is well spent. The activities that involve a skit will require additional time to prepare the participants.

Above all, have fun helping the children find a God and a church that are alive!

Part One

Advent and Christmas

Gifts From Jesus

Scripture: 1 Corinthians 1:3–9
(First Sunday of Advent — B)

Preparation:

■ Wrap small blocks of wood in Christmas paper, tie them with ribbon, and attach the following message:

> Here is a gift just for you from me.
> It's so special that you never unwrap it.
> Yet, I bet you will discover
> that this gift keeps appearing
> wrapped in many different packages
> — parents, friends, puppies, kittens, flowers. . .
> That's because the gift I give to you
> is my love for *you*.
>
> So put this present where you can see it,
> hold it when you want to, and remember:
> I LOVE YOU.
>
> Jesus

■ Make a big envelope out of poster board; address it to the children from Jesus. Put the following letter, written on big sheets of paper, inside:

> Dear Students,
>
> On Christmas we will celebrate my birthday. It is fun to celebrate with you. You really have a good time.
>
> But sometimes I feel left out. Everyone is excited and giving gifts to each other, but they don't always notice the gifts I have given them. Maybe you don't get excited because I haven't wrapped them in brightly colored paper.
>
> This year I want to give you a brightly wrapped gift. This gift is so special that you don't even need

to open it. Read the card attached to the gift and you will understand.

I am looking forward to celebrating with you on Christmas.

Love,
Jesus

Homily Text:

What are some ways we remember people who live far away? *(phone calls, letters, cards...)* Our reading today is part of one of the letters St. Paul wrote to the followers of Jesus. He often wrote letters like this to remind people that Jesus loved them.

Sometimes it's hard to remember all the good things Jesus does for us because he isn't right here with us. That's why during Advent we remember that Jesus is Emmanuel, a name that means "God with us."

At Christmas time especially we get cards from friends and relatives that we don't always see. Today let's imagine that Jesus has written us a Christmas letter. *(Ask two children to hold the letter. Read the letter aloud.)*

The letter says we have gifts from Jesus so we better pass them out. First I want to remind you that Jesus said not to open these gifts. *(Pass out the gifts and read the tag aloud.)*

This present reminds us that Jesus loves us. His love shows up in packages like moms and dads, brothers and sisters, friends and classmates. Jesus wants to be with us as we exchange gifts this Christmas, because he is the greatest gift of all.

Put this present on your Christmas tree, on the mantel above your fireplace, on your dresser, or anywhere else you will see it often. And remember: Jesus loves you.

Add Vent

Scripture: 1 Thessalonians 3:12 — 4:2
(First Sunday of Advent — C)

Preparation:

■ You will need a paper plate to demonstrate the "vent."

■ Make a poster that says, "Add Vent."

Homily Text:

What season of the church year are we in now? *(Advent)* What is Advent? *(Explain to the students that "advent" means coming. It refers to Christ's coming as a baby in Bethlehem, his coming to us now, and his final coming at the end of the world.)* What do we do during Advent? *(Advent is the time when we prepare our hearts to have Jesus dwell with us.)*

What does it sound like when you say "Advent"? *(add vent; show sign)* If we think about those two words, "add vent," we can get a better idea of what this season is all about.

What does a vent do? *(lets air in and out)* Where do we find vents? *(ceilings, roofs, cars)* Let's pretend we're going to add a vent to our lives. I need one volunteer. *(Give the volunteer a paper plate to use as a "vent" on the top of his or her head. The volunteer lifts up the plate to let something in or out.)* Now we have a vent. What would we want to let out of our lives during Advent?. . . What would we want to let into our lives during Advent?. . .

This Advent add a vent to your life. Let out those things in your life that lead you away from God and add in those things that lead you to God. Then you will be ready to celebrate Jesus' birthday at Christmas.

Have You Checked Your "Oil" Lately?

Scripture: 1 Thessalonians 5:16–24
(Third Sunday of Advent — B)

Preparation:

■ You will need a can of STP Oil Treatment and a can that says "JTP Life Treatment" (write "Joyful," "Thankful," and "Prayerful" on the back of the can).

■ Make a poster that says, "Have you checked your "oil" lately?"

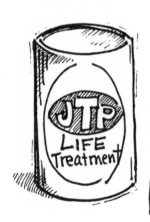

Have you checked your oil lately?

Homily Text:

What does our poster say today?...What do we check oil in?...Why do we check the oil?...Our cars and machines can run fine with regular oil in them. Some people, though, add STP Oil Treatment to their oil to make it work better, to protect the engine. *(Hold up can of STP Oil Treatment.)*

   We could say that we have "oil" in us, but it's not the kind of oil we use in cars and machines. The oil that keeps us running smoothly is our life in Jesus. How can we keep this "oil" working its best? We need something like JTP Life Treatment. *(Hold up can of JTP Life Treatment.)* What do you think "JTP" stands for? *(joyful, thankful, prayerful)*

In our reading Paul says that joyfulness, thankfulness, and prayerfulness should be part of our lives. We need to check and make sure that they are. If not, we need to add some JTP Life Treatment: add some joy, thanks, and prayer.

We don't have to use STP Oil Treatment. Regular oil works just fine. But for Christians, joyfulness, thankfulness, and prayerfulness have to be our way of life. We don't have a choice about using JTP Life Treatment.

The next time you or your parents check the oil in your car, lawn mower, snowblower, or tractor, take a few minutes to check your own "oil" and see if you need any JTP Life Treatment.

Jesus Is the Light in Our Lives

Scripture: Luke 1:26b–35, 38
(Fourth Sunday of Advent — B)

Preparation:

■ You will need candles that relight on their own, two regular candles, and clay to put candles in so they're easy to hold.

Homily Text:

(Light a candle that will relight.) Candles are used a lot in our church. Do you know why? *(a sign of Jesus, who is the light of the world)* What candles do you see? *(When a candle in the church is pointed out, ask the children if they know what it is for. This helps them understand the uses and symbolism of the different candles.)*

What kind of a candle am I holding today? *(birthday candle)* Why would I be holding a birthday candle? *(We will be celebrating Jesus' birthday soon.)* This is a special birthday candle. We need a special one because Jesus is so special. When I blow out this candle *(blow it out)*, it relights. This candle reminds us that Jesus' light will never go out.

Jesus' light came into the world when Mary said yes to God. We each have a light in us — Jesus' life. Our light is different than Jesus'. It can be blown out. *(Have two children come to the front and hold regular candles. Have one of the children blow out his or her candle.)*

Our lights go out when we say no to God. We can relight our candles by saying yes to God. We can also discover God in friends and family and other people we meet and relight our candle from theirs. *(Have the child relight his or her candle from the other child's candle.)*

Remember to say yes to God as Mary did and keep your light burning. *(Note: Blow out the candle that relights several times during the lesson. The children love the effect and I believe it makes the message clearer.)*

Trust Like Mary

Scripture: Luke 1:39–45
              (Fourth Sunday of Advent — C)

Preparation:

■ Choose two or three adults or older students to help; explain their roles to them before the activity begins.

Homily Text:

(Begin by asking the adults or older students to come forward. Ask for two or three other volunteers from the younger students. Explain that each smaller person is to stand in front of a bigger person [back facing the bigger person]. One at a time have each smaller person fall backward — trusting the person behind to catch him or her. Have all the people return to their seats.)

What happened? Did the people in front look like they felt comfortable falling? . . . Why would it be hard to fall back into someone's arms like that? *(not sure they will catch you)* *(Ask the smaller volunteers:)* Why did you trust the people behind you to catch you? . . .

It is hard to trust that someone will catch you. You know it will hurt to fall to the ground and you don't know for sure that the person is strong enough, is paying attention, or even wants to catch you.

This kind of trust is similar to the trust that Mary had. When did Mary have to trust? *(when asked to be the Mother of God, when she and Joseph were raising Jesus, when Jesus was lost in the Temple, when Jesus was crucified . . .)* When Mary trusted God, it didn't mean no one would make fun of her or that she wouldn't have to face a lot of pain in her life. Why do you think Mary decided to trust God? . . . *(She would always have God's help when things were difficult.)*

When Mary went to visit Elizabeth, Elizabeth said, "Blessed is she who trusted that the Lord's words to her would be fulfilled." What a wonderful compliment to give anyone!

We are to trust like Mary did. We are to believe that God will take care of us and be with us through everything in our lives. I hope that someday someone can say to you, "Blessed are *(fill in several of the children's names)* who trusted that the Lord's words to them would be fulfilled."

Follow the Star

Scripture: Matthew 2:1–12 (Feast of Epiphany)

Preparation:

■ Cut little stars out of construction paper. You will also need a marker and masking tape.

■ Make a poster that says, "Follow THE Star."

Homily Text:

How many of you would follow a star like the three kings did?...
Would you leave everything behind, not knowing where you were going, not knowing when you would get there, not knowing what you
would find?

When the kings followed the star they risked a lot. They might
have lost their kingdoms, or even their lives. They knew that this
was a special star, one that announced the birth of the king of kings.
This made it worthwhile to follow the star no matter what.

Besides the stars in the night sky, what else do you think of when
I say "star"? *(movie stars, basketball stars, rock stars...)* Name some
of these stars... Have any of you written to them?... Do you have
posters of any of them?... Are you members of their fan clubs?...

Do you or your friends follow these stars?... Why? *(cute, famous, want to be like them...)*

The kings remind us that some stars are more worth following than others. What would be some stars that are worth following in your lives? *(dreams, goals, the Bible...) (Write the children's responses on the little stars and add them to the poster.)* If you choose your little stars carefully, they will all lead you closer to Jesus.

Today, be like the three kings. Follow the star to Jesus, the light of our lives.

Part Two
Lent

Which Body Are You?

Scripture: 2 Corinthians 5:20 — 6:2
(Note: This lesson is designed for Ash Wednesday)

Preparation:

■ Make a paper body with attachable hair and facial features. Also make small signs that say blood, bones, skin, muscles. Bring in a skeleton or a picture of a skeleton.

Homily Text:

What is your body made of? . . . *(show the body and add signs as they mention parts and features)* What can your body do? *(With the body, demonstrate some of the things the children say.)* What is something your body can't do that someone else's can? *(splits . . .)*

After we die, our bodies become like this skeleton. What can a skeleton do? *(nothing)* There is nothing to hold the bones together. There are no muscles to make them move.

Today you will receive ashes on your forehead. Where do these ashes come from? *(Last year's palms were burned to make the ashes.)* The ashes are put on your forehead in the form of a cross. Why? *(as a reminder of Jesus' death)* These ashes remind us that we will all die someday and be dust and ashes.

Why does the church want to remind us about death? . . . At the beginning of Lent, we remember that while we're alive, we need to make sure our lives are like Jesus' life. Then when we die, we will have the life with God that Jesus promised.

This Lent you have a choice. You can be a body that is active and trying to become more like God. You can be alive and growing in your relationship with God. Or you can be a skeleton, doing nothing to open yourself to God. It's your choice. Which are you going to be?

The Lenten Snake

Scripture: Galatians 2:19b–20

Preparation:

■ You might want to make a stuffed snake with removable skin
to demonstrate this lesson. (I used scraps of material to make
a snake and then stuffed it. Then I made another snake,
slightly bigger than the previous one. This is the "removable
skin." Put it on the snake.) Or you might want to bring in a
picture of a snake shedding its skin. The more adventurous
might like to bring in an actual snake skin!

Homily Text:

How many of you like snakes? . . . Not too many of you. *(Homilist can
share a personal reaction to snakes. I told the children that I've always liked snakes because my dad was a science teacher so we had
snakes around when I was growing up.)*

Today I'm interested in the snake's skin. Do you know how snakes
shed their skins? . . . A snake starts shedding its skin by loosening
the skin around its mouth. *(Begin to take the skin off of the stuffed
snake. Slowly pull the snake out of the skin. You might want to do
this gradually throughout the homily.)* When the old skin is gone, the
new skin is bright and clean and shiny.

Why does a snake shed its skin? *(So it can grow.)* During Lent
each year we have a chance to grow and become more like God's children. We are like a snake shedding its skin. We give up things and
try to change bad habits. We shed things that we've outgrown, like
pouting and temper tantrums when we don't get our way, or lying
when we've done something wrong. Each time we get rid of a bad
habit and replace it with something good, it's like getting rid of an
old, tight skin so we can grow.

Today let's think about what things we can shed this Lent so that
we can bring a bright new self to God on Easter.

Pray Always

Scripture: Ephesians 6:18b–19
(Note: This lesson can be used during Lent to talk about prayer.)

Preparation:

■ Make a big pretzel made out of construction paper.

■ Put pretzels in plastic bags and attach a tag with the following message:

> There is a legend about a monk who made altar breads. One day he had leftover dough so he shaped the dough into dolls. Their arms were crossed in prayer. The monk gave these dolls to children as a reminder to pray. These breads were later called pretzels.
>
> Lent is a special time of prayer.
>
> The pretzel reminds us to pray.

Homily Text:

What was the reading about? *(pray always)* Do any of you do that? Why not? What does it mean to pray always? . . . It doesn't mean spending all our time kneeling down with our hands folded, saying lots of prayers. We can pray always by asking God's help, thanking God for good things that happen, even praising God just because we're alive and healthy. Praying always also means being aware that God is always present in our hearts and in the people around us.

Sometimes we need to be reminded to pray. We can use a pretzel to remind us. Pretzels began as an ancient tradition for Lent. *(Share the legend about why pretzels were first made. Tell the children that people used to cross their arms on their chests when praying. Use the big pretzel to show the children how it resembles arms crossed in prayer.)*

Today I have a pretzel for each of you. Take it home and put it on your refrigerator or table to remind you to pray during Lent. Wait until Easter to eat it.

And, remember, pray always.

Help Wanted

Scripture: 1 Samuel 16:1–13
               (Fourth Sunday of Lent — A)
               Psalm 89

Preparation:

- Lean a big cross against the altar or in front of the class-room with the words "I have found my servants" on it.

- Make a poster that says, "Help Wanted: Children to help carry Jesus' Cross."

- Have each person write his or her name on a small piece of paper. You will also need a supply of thumbtacks.

Note:

I dressed as a clown for this homily/lesson and used the following introduction. I used a newspaper with the "Help Wanted" poster on a large sheet of newsprint in the middle of the classified section.

"Oh look, a newspaper. Just what I need. I am looking for a job. It's really hard to find a job for a clown *(flip through the want ads)*. . . I haven't found a job for a clown, but here is an interesting ad. It's really big. *(Show the children the poster.)*. . . *(Continue with "What do you think it means to carry Jesus' cross?". . .)*

Homily Text:

How many of you have seen "help wanted" signs in stores and restaurants? We have a sign of our own today. *(Hold up the "Help Wanted" sign and read what it says.)* What do you think it means to carry Jesus' cross? . . . Here's a cross. How many students would we need to carry this one? *(Answers will depend on the size of the cross.)* Do you think this is what it means? What are other ways we can carry crosses? *(carry love to others, help others, be patient when we have something difficult to do . . .)*

In our first reading today, David was chosen to follow God's call. It wasn't easy. Maybe you've heard the story about David fighting a giant with only a sling shot. He won because he had faith in God, but he was scared because Goliath was so much bigger and stronger and more powerful than David.

It isn't easy to be a follower of Jesus, either. That's why we talk about carrying his cross. During Lent we can do things that will make us stronger spiritually, so that we can help Jesus carry his cross. We need one another to help us do these things. And we need God to help strengthen us.

Think about something you can do between now and Easter to help Jesus carry his cross. Then come forward with the piece of paper that has your name on it. Put it on the cross with a thumbtack as a sign that you want to follow Jesus.

I Lost My...

Scripture: Luke 15:11–24
             (Fourth Sunday of Lent — C)

Preparation:

■   Make two posters:

> Lost
> Brown, Male, Irish Setter
> Belongs to very sad children
> Please help him
> find his home.

> Lost
> My younger son
> Please tell him his father loves him very much
> and hopes he will come home soon.

Homily Text:

Have any of you ever lost a pet?... What did you do to find your pet?... Some of you may have put up a sign like this. *(read sign about Irish setter)* Why do you look for lost pets?... Do you look for them even if they chew up your shoes or get into the trash?... Why? *(because you love them)*

What is today's gospel about?... The father could have made a sign like this. *(Show the "younger son" poster and read it aloud.)* The father wanted his son to know he loves him no matter what he did.

Jesus tells this story in the gospel to show us how much God loves all his children. He wants us to know that any time we feel lost, any time we've done something wrong, God will always welcome us home because he loves us.

Breaking Out of
Our Shells

Scripture: Matthew 26:14–25
(Palm Sunday — A [partial])

Preparation:

■ You will need a plastic egg (the bigger it is the better). Cut eggs out of different colors of construction paper. Have each person write his or her name on a paper egg before the activity begins.

■ Make a poster that says, "Break out of your shells!"

Homily Text:

Eggs are one symbol of Easter. What do they stand for? *(new life)* To help us better understand that, let's pretend that this plastic egg I am holding is big enough for you to get in. What is it like inside? . . . What does it feel like to have a shell around you? . . .

Judas was in an egg. His shell was invisible, just like the one you're in right now. It was made from a desire for money, for material things. His shell prevented him from seeing all that Jesus had to offer.

We all have shells around us. What do you think your shell could be made of? *(sins, thinking only of self, too much TV, ignoring other people . . .)* Part of our job during Lent is to try to break our shell from the inside so that on Easter we can celebrate our new life. How do you think we might do that? *(do things for others, give up something that we want but really don't need . . .)* When we pray we can ask Jesus to help break the shell that's around us.

Bring up the paper egg that has your name on it and put it on this sign. *(Read the sign.)* This will remind us to break out of our shells and celebrate our new life with Jesus.

Part Three

Easter and Pentecost

"Piece" Be With You

Scripture: John 20:19–23 (Second Sunday of Easter — A, B, or C
[partial])

Preparation:

■   Paint lines on a piece of construction paper to make the paper
look like a puzzle. Paint "YOU" on this paper. Cut out the
center of the "O" in "YOU." Put the puzzle picture on a sign
that says, "'Piece' be with you."

■   Make four puzzle pieces: three do not fit the center of the "O"
in YOU; they have "FOOD," "TV," and "MONEY" written on
them. One puzzle piece fits the center of the "O." It has "GOD"
written on it.

Homily Text:

What is wrong with this sign? *(Center of "O" is missing, "peace" is
spelled wrong.)* What does this "piece" mean? What did Jesus mean
when he said, "Peace be with you"?... He was giving us himself because he is peace in the fullest sense. He makes us whole.

This is hard to understand. Maybe this will help. Inside of us we
have a space that we might call our "God space." It isn't a space we
can see. To help us imagine it, I've made this poster. We need to fill

the center of the word "YOU" with a piece (p-i-e-c-e) that's the right shape. We'll say that this "O" is our "God space."

When we're hungry, we feel like we have a hollow space in our stomachs. What do we fill that with? *(food)* Will food fill our "God space"? *(Hold up the puzzle piece with "FOOD" written on it. The piece obviously doesn't fit into the center of the "O.")* When we're bored, we fill up our time with lots of activity, like watching TV. Does TV fill our "God space"? *(Hold up puzzle piece with "TV" written on it.)* Does it fit? *(no)* Sometimes we think that if we just had money to buy clothes and toys like everyone else, we will be happy. We think this will fill us up. *(Hold up puzzle piece with "MONEY" written on it.)* Does it fit? *(no)*

What do you think we need to fill our "God space" with? *(God. Hold up puzzle piece with "GOD" written on it)* Does it fit? *(yes)* When Jesus says, "Peace be with you," he wants to fill us with God's love and peace. He is asking us to keep our God space open for God. Then we can let his peace fill our space and complete the puzzle we are.

Follow the Yellow Brick Road

Scripture: Luke 24:13–35
(Third Sunday of Easter — A)

Preparation:

■ Make a poster that says, "Follow the Yellow Brick Road."

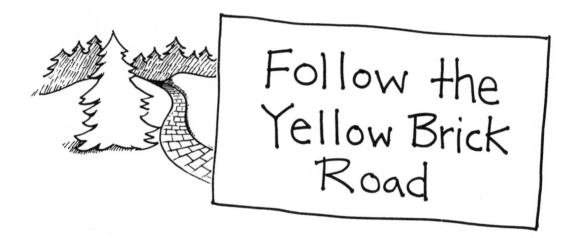

Homily Text:

What does our sign say today? *(Follow the yellow brick road.)* Where have you heard that before? *(The Wizard of Oz)* Who was following the yellow brick road? *(Dorothy, Toto, Tin Man, Scarecrow, and Lion)* Where were they going? *(to see the wizard of Oz)* Why were they going to see the wizard? *(They thought the wizard could help Dorothy and Toto get back to Kansas, the Lion have courage, the Tin Man to get a heart, and the Scarecrow to get a brain.)* When they found out the wizard couldn't grant their wishes, he explained to them that they already had the gifts of knowledge and love and courage, but they just didn't realize it.

It could be said that the disciples on the road to Emmaus were on a "yellow brick road." They were trying to figure out what they would do now that their friend and teacher had been killed. Who was the stranger on the road to Emmaus? *(Jesus)* When Jesus came along, he explained to them what the Bible taught and what it meant in their lives. They had heard these things before but now they understood.

We're on a "yellow brick road," too. Where does it lead? *(heaven)* Who are the companions on our journey? *(friends, family)* We meet other people on our way, like the disciples did on the road to Emmaus. These people might be teachers, priests, and other people who tell us about God and Jesus.

We don't have to wait till the end of the road to find God. God is with us always. Today we are challenged to walk our "yellow brick road" and discover how God walks with us every day in the people who love us and teach us and bring us closer to Jesus.

Which Shepherd
Do You Follow?

Scripture: John 10:11–16
(Fourth Sunday of Easter — B)

Preparation:

■ Divide the children into five groups as they enter by giving each one a piece of paper with a number between 1 and 5 written on it.
Make signs that say:

Shepherd #1 — Stylish

Shepherd #2 — Money

Shepherd #3 — Me

Shepherd #4 — Jesus

■ Ask four people to hold the shepherd signs; explain their roles to them before the activity begins.

Homily Text:

I want to welcome all of you to a meeting of sheep from all over the country. They represent four major groups of sheep. Let's meet the shepherds who lead these flocks.

Shepherd #1, identify yourself. *(Child comes forward with sign and says, "I am Shepherd #1. My name is Stylish." Repeat this for the other three shepherds.)*

Now let's meet the sheep who belong to these shepherds' flocks. The sheep in Shepherd #1's flock — Stylish's flock — raise your hands. *(All children with a #1 should raise their hands. Repeat this for all the flocks.)*

We also have some other sheep here. Number 5's, please raise your hands. These sheep are here to decide which shepherd they want to follow. What does a shepherd do? *(At Jesus' time, all the sheep of a village were kept in the same place at night and taken to pasture each day. Shepherds called their sheep by name. A good shepherd knew where to find plenty of good grass and water for the sheep. Shepherds risked their lives to save the sheep from wolves, bears, and lions.)*

Now let's hear how these shepherds call their sheep. What do you think Shepherd #1, Stylish, would say to get his sheep to follow him? *("Everybody's got it"... "This is the latest fashion."...)*

(Repeat this for the other three shepherds, spending the most time on what Jesus would say. Use ideas such as these, adapting them to messages the children will understand: Come to me, you who are weary; love one another as I have loved you; peace be with you....)

Group #5, do you know which shepherd you want to follow? What about all of you other sheep? Are you happy with your shepherds? Do you think they'll take care of you the way a shepherd should?

Sometimes we are tempted to follow people who don't watch over us and take care of us. Sometimes they lead us into bad places. Our challenge is to keep Jesus as our shepherd. We are to follow him as he calls us by name.

Today, think about this question: "Which shepherd do you follow?"

Are You Following Your Compass?

Scripture: John 14:1–12
(Fifth Sunday of Easter — A)

Preparation:

■ Make two compasses out of cardboard. You could also bring in a real compass.

Homily Text:

I want you to think about your home and all the streets and roads around it. Think of the route you take from school to your home.... Now think of the route your parents take from work.... the route you'll take home from church today... the route from the grocery store... the route from a friend's house...

We can take many routes to our homes. The same is true for the house Jesus has prepared for us. We all have a different route, a different life path to take. But, we all follow the same way — Jesus' way.

To find our way in an area we are not familiar with we use a compass. *(Show the regular compass.)* How does a compass work? *(The needle points to the north... the needle points to the magnetic field at the North Pole.)* If you know which way is north, you can use a map to find your way.

Sometimes things happen in our lives that are new and unfamiliar. What might some of these things be? *(moving... new friends... beginning a new school year...)* It helps to know that Jesus is with us to help us at these times. We have a compass within us that points to Jesus' way. *(Show the "Jesus' Way" compass.)*

We have to take care of a compass. If it is dropped or stepped on, it won't be accurate. It won't point us in the right direction. The same is true for the compass within us. How can we keep this compass accurate? *(read the Bible, listen to other people who follow Jesus, pray . . .)*

Our gospel today tells us Jesus is the Way, the Truth, and the Life. If we keep our compass set on Jesus' way then someday we will arrive at the place Jesus has prepared for us.

Mirror, Mirror

Scripture: 1 John 5:1–6

(Second Sunday of Easter — B)

1 John 4:7–10 (Sixth Sunday of Easter — B)

1 John 4:11–16 (Seventh Sunday of Easter — B)

Note: This lesson can also be used to teach the children about Christian witness in the world.

Preparation:

■ On heavy paper or cardboard make a drawing that represents the body's circulatory system and label it "Our Christ-Veins."

Homily Text:

How many of you have heard the saying, "Mirror, mirror on the wall, who's the fairest of them all?" . . .

Today I'd like to pretend that we have a magical mirror. This mirror doesn't show us what color our hair is, or whether there is mud on our faces. Instead, it shows us whether we are being Christ-like. Here's an example of what someone might look like in our magical mirror. *(Hold up the cardboard body.)*

What does this look like to you? *(our veins, where our blood flows)* Yes, except with our magical mirror these are our Christ-veins. If we could look at someone's Christ-veins, we could tell whether they are being Christ-like.

For example, let's imagine what Mother Teresa's Christ-veins would look like. Who is Mother Teresa? *(a nun who takes care of the poorest of the poor in India and other places)* If she were to look in our magical mirror, do you think she'd see the fluid in her Christ-veins not moving, barely moving, or moving rapidly? *(moving rapidly)* Why? *(She is doing what Christ would do — caring for the needy.)*

How about Martin Luther King, Jr.? What did he do? *(He was an American civil rights leader who tried to bring about equal rights for blacks in peaceful ways.)* How would the fluid in his Christ-veins be moving? *(rapidly)* Why?

(You might want to ask about other people they might know in their families, school, or parish.)

How about the fluid in your Christ-veins? Is it moving? My guess is that it is. How fast or how slow the fluid is moving depends on how much you are like Christ. Why is it important to be Christ-like? *(Jesus asks us to, good example for others, helps others be Christ-like...)*

The next time you look in a mirror, pretend it is a magical mirror. Pretend that you can see your Christ-veins and ask, "Mirror, mirror on the wall, is my Christ-fluid moving at all?" Try to make it move fast all day by being Christ-like to yourself and other people.

Up, Up, and Away

Scripture: Acts 1:1–11 (Ascension)

Preparation:

■ You will need two balloons filled with helium. Tie a string or ribbon to each and then attach clear thread or fishing line to the string or ribbon.

■ Make a small sign (to fit on one of the balloons) that says "Jesus." You will also need masking tape to attach the sign to the balloon.

Homily Text:

(Hold the two balloons by the string or ribbon.) How many of you have ever had a helium balloon?... How many of you have ever accidently let go of the string on a helium balloon or seen a young child do this?... *(Let go of one of the balloons. The clear thread will allow you to retrieve it later.)* What does the child do when he or she realizes what has happened? *(cries, tries to catch it, wants another balloon...)*

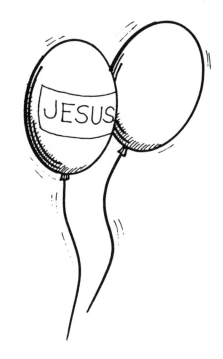

What are we celebrating today? *(Ascension, Jesus' rising into heaven)* Let's pretend that this balloon is Jesus. *(With masking tape put the Jesus sign on the second balloon.)* At the Ascension, Jesus was lifted up in a cloud and then the people could no longer see him: sort of like letting go of a helium balloon. *(Release the balloon labeled "Jesus.")* If we were outside the balloon would soon be gone from our sight. The apostles may have felt like a young child who lost his or her balloon: trying to find Jesus, wanting him back, perhaps even crying because he was gone.

Two angels came and told the apostles that Jesus will return. (Pull down the Jesus' balloon by the clear thread.) The hope that Jesus will return keeps us working to build God's kingdom and trying to be more like Christ. This way we will be ready when he returns.

Happy Birthday to Us!

Scripture: Acts 2:1–13 (Pentecost)

Preparation:

■ You will need a candle that will relight on its own, a piece of clay to stick the candle in, matches, and sheets of paper with "Happy Birthday" written on them in the following languages:

Latin: **Felicem natalem tibi!**

German: **Herzlichen Glückwunsch zum Geburtstag**

French: **Bon Anniversaire**

Spanish: **Feliz cumpleaños**

English: **Happy Birthday**

Chinese: 生日快樂

Russian: **С днём рождения**

Homily Text:

What is today? *(Pentecost)* What's that? *(the coming of the Holy Spirit)* Did you know that it's also a birthday? Whose birthday do you think it is? *(the church)* What's the church? *(We are the church.)* So, it is our birthday!! Did anyone bring a birthday cake? . . . I forgot one, but I did remember a candle. *(pick up the piece of clay)* We can put the candle in this.

Now we need to decide what language to sing "Happy Birthday" in. Why do you think I say that? *(On Pentecost, people who spoke many different languages heard the apostles speaking in their own languages.)* We could sing "Happy Birthday" in . . . *(Show a card and let the children guess what language it is. Do this for all the languages.)*

We better sing in English so everyone can sing. *(Light the candle.)* These are the words we will use:

> "Happy birthday to us,
> happy birthday to us,
> happy birthday dear church,
> happy birthday to us."

(Sing "Happy Birthday." Have a child blow out the candle. When it relights, have another child blow the candle out.) Why do you think the candle won't stay out? . . . Yes, it's one of those candles that won't stay blown out. Why would we use that kind of a candle to celebrate the church's birthday? *(reminds us that the Holy Spirit is always with the church, with us)*

We have a lot to celebrate on Pentecost. We have been given the most wonderful gift: the gift of God's Spirit to be with us always.

The Holy Spirit

Scripture: Acts 2:1–13 (Pentecost)

Preparation:

■   You will need a fan and extension cord, a pile of papers, a blown-up balloon, and a balloon not blown up.

Homily Text:

In today's reading, the Holy Spirit is described as being like a "strong, driving wind." In other places in the Bible, we hear how the Holy Spirit is like a gentle breeze. If the Holy Spirit is like the wind then we can look at the wind to find out what the Holy Spirit is like.

Let's pretend that this fan is the wind. *(Point the fan at a pile of papers.)* What does the wind do to a pile of papers? *(moves and spreads them)* What does the Holy Spirit move and spread? *(moves our hearts to God, spreads God's love, spreads the good news . . .)*

(Point the fan at a blown-up balloon.) What does the wind do to a balloon? *(lifts it into the air)* What does the Holy Spirit lift? *(lifts our spirits, lifts our hearts to God . . .)*

Now imagine that your breath is the wind. *(Ask one of the children to blow up a balloon.)* What does the breath do to the balloon? *(expands it)* Our breath expands a balloon. What does the Holy Spirit expand or make bigger? *(helps us to love more, gives us a greater desire for God . . .)*

(Ask the child to let go of the balloon while it is still blown up. The balloon will go all over.) Is the wind inside of the balloon predictable or unpredictable? Do you know what it is going to do? *(no)* Is the Holy Spirit unpredictable? *(Yes, the Spirit can act in our lives in surprising ways, such as giving us the courage to help a boy no one likes.)*

How is the wind blowing today? Sometimes the wind is gentle. Other times it is forceful and strong. Is the Holy Spirit that way? *(yes)* How? . . .

Let's pretend it is a very hot day, and _____ *(use one of the children's names)* goes outside. *(Point the fan at the child.)* What will the wind do for her? *(cool her off, refresh her)* The Holy Spirit was

Jesus' gift to the apostles. The Holy Spirit gave them the extra help they needed to tell the world about God and Jesus. The Holy Spirit is also Jesus' gift to us. The Holy Spirit is with us all the time.

The next time you feel the wind, stop and think, "Am I letting the Holy Spirit move, spread, lift, refresh, and expand within me?"

Part Four
Sundays of the Year

Jesus' Net

Scripture: Luke 5:1–11 (Fifth Sunday of the Year — C)
Matthew 4:12–23 (Third Sunday of the Year — A)
Mark 1:14–20 (Third Sunday of the Year — B)

Preparation:

■ Cut out fish of different colors of construction paper. Have the children write their names on the paper fish as they come in.

■ Make a poster that says, "We are caught in Jesus' net."

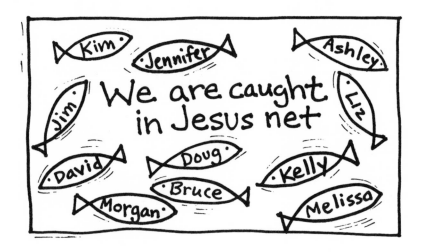

Homily Text:

What does a fish look like?... *(fins, tail, scales... Have the children pretend to be fish as they mention these things.)* Where do fish live? *(in water)* Who went fishing this summer? What do you do when you fish? *(catch fish)* Fish aren't always safe in the water. What could be dangerous? *(nets, hooks...)*

Let's say you're a fish and you get caught in a net. What could happen to you? *(could be eaten...)* Something good could happen. You could be caught in a net and put in an aquarium. You would be safe there.

In our gospel Jesus told James and John that they would be fishers of people. They would catch people in Jesus' net — an invisible net. Getting caught in Jesus' net means living the way Jesus asks us to.

Let's always let Jesus catch us in his net. Let's be Jesus' fish by living according to Jesus' way. *(Have the children tape their fish to the poster.)*

Be a Butterfly

Scripture: Luke 9:18–24 (Twelfth Sunday of the Year — C)

Preparation:

■ Make a caterpillar, cocoon, and butterfly out of construction paper. You will need masking tape to attach them to the poster.

■ Make a poster that says, "Be a Butterfly."

Homily Text:

How many of you have seen a caterpillar?... *(Hold up the caterpillar.)* What do caterpillars do? *(eat and eat and eat)* When a caterpillar is too big for its skin, what happens? *(sheds the skin)* Then the caterpillar eats some more. Eventually the caterpillar is through eating. Then what happens? *(Sheds its skin for the last time and turns into a chrysalis or spins a cocoon — hold up cocoon.)* Then what happens? *(after a certain amount of time the caterpillars come out as moths or butterflies — hold up the butterfly)*

The same is true for you and me. No, you won't become a moth or butterfly, but you can become more than you are now.

We call some people saints. Do you know why? *(They lived good lives, they prayed a lot, they healed people, they were especially like Jesus . . . .)* Can you name some saints? . . . These people were caterpillars, like you and me. They ate, slept, prayed, studied, played, worked. . . . There was one thing different about them. They weren't afraid to take the extra step and become a butterfly *(hold up the butterfly)* to follow God. Many of them risked a lot, even their lives, to follow God. Because of this the church recognizes them as saints: people who are examples to us of how to live the Christian life.

(You might want to give an example by discussing a favorite saint, the patron saint of the parish, etc. Ask:) What was this saint like when he (she) was a caterpillar? . . . a butterfly? . . .

Which Balloon Are You?

Scripture: Matthew 13:1–23
(Fifteenth Sunday of the Year — A)

Preparation:

■ You will need four balloons on balloon holders — red balloon filled with helium; orange balloon almost fully blown up with air; yellow balloon halfway blown up with air; blue balloon not blown up — and two balloons, one yellow and one orange, not blown up.

Note:
I dressed as a clown for this one. If you would like to do this, the following remarks serve as a good introduction.

"Good morning. As long as I can remember I've wanted to be a clown. And, as you can see, I got to be a clown. I wanted to be a clown that carries balloons. And I got to do that, too. But my balloons are different than other clown balloons. What is different about them?" *(not blown up all the way)*

Homily Text:

I have four balloons today and they're all different colors. They're supposed to remind us of something. Let's take the blue balloon. What could it remind you of?... Today it reminds us of those people who hear God's word, who see God all around them, but still ignore God. They walk away and forget all about him.

What about the yellow balloon?... It reminds us of those who hear God's Word and let God come into their lives a little, but then quickly forget him. *(Blow up another yellow balloon and let the air out of it to demonstrate this.)*

And the orange balloon?... Some people hear God's Word and live it for a while *(blow up a balloon)* and then slowly forget God. They forget that God is with them when they play. They forget God is with them at school. *(Slowly let a little air out of the balloon with each statement until all the air is released.)* Eventually they have forgotten God.

The red balloon?... The red balloon is for those who hear God and see God and remember that God is with them and try to live according to God's ways. The enthusiasm never goes out of them.

How is this like the gospel reading? *(Help the students make the connection with the seeds that fell in different kinds of ground.)*

Imagine that you are a balloon. Which balloon are you?... Are you the blue one? *(Hold up each balloon as its color is mentioned.)* The yellow one? The orange one? Or the red one? Let's remember to always try to be the red balloon.

Let's Be Like Honeybees

Scripture: John 6:1–15
(Seventeenth Sunday of the Year — B)

Homily Text:

Today let's imagine that we are honeybees. What does a honeybee look like? *(wings, yellow and black stripes, antennae . . . Have the children pretend to be honeybees by putting on the characteristics they name.)* What do honeybees do? *(make honey)* How do they do this? *(get pollen from flowers)* What else do honeybees do? *(take care of the baby honeybees, protect the hive)* Each honeybee has a job to do. Some get pollen while others protect the hive and others take care of the babies. *(You might want to have the children pretend to fly around to get pollen.)*

The little boy in today's gospel had a special job to do, too. What did he do? *(gave Jesus the bread and fish)* If this little boy hadn't given Jesus the bread and fish, Jesus wouldn't have been able to perform the miracle the way he did.

We all have important jobs to do. What are some of your jobs? *(going to school, helping around the house . . .)* How does this help Jesus? *(He told us that when we do good things for others, we're doing it for him.)*

God calls us to be like honeybees, or to be like the boy in today's story. We are called to do our job in God's family.

Taking Time for God

Scripture: Luke 11:1–13
(Seventeenth Sunday of the Year — C)

Preparation:

■ Ask six people to act out the skit. You will also need a basketball and a telephone for props.

Homily Text:

(Athlete is busy practicing basketball, tossing and bouncing the ball.)

Character #1: Hey, Athlete! I just got a new Nintendo game. Come play it with me.

Athlete: Can't you tell I am practicing for the game this week? I don't have time right now to play. I'll play with you as soon as I can. *(Character #1 walks off.)*

Character #2: Let's go fishing, Athlete. Dad said I have the whole day free.

Athlete: Not right now. I need to practice. I'll go fishing with you later. *(Character #2 walks off.)*

Character #3: Athlete, do you have that fifty cents you borrowed to buy a pop?

Athlete: It's in the house. I'll get it for you later. *(Character #3 walks off.)*

Character #4: It's Saturday. It's time to work on our science experiment for next week.

Athlete: I forgot all about it. It will just have to wait. I need to practice some more. *(Character #4 walks off.)*

Character #5: Mom said it is time for you to set the table.

Athlete: Won't you do it for me? I really need to practice.

Character #5: No! It's your turn. *(Character #5 walks off.)*

Athlete:	*(Athlete continues to practice for a while.)* *(The phone rings.)* There's the phone. *(Athlete answers the phone.)* Hello . . . . Who is this? . . . Jesus? . . . Are you kidding me? . . . So you really are Jesus? . . . Yes, you're right. It has been a long time since I took the time to say good morning or good night to you . . . . No, I haven't told you about my days lately . . . . You must have been waiting a long time for me, Jesus. . . .Yes, I guess I have been too busy with my basketball to take time for other people—playing with them, helping them, doing my chores. . . . Sure I'll let you be a part of my life again. I'll spend some time with you in prayer, and I'll go look for those people who needed me earlier. *(Athlete walks off carrying the phone.)*
Homilist:	Athlete realized he hadn't been talking to God lately. He hadn't been praying. What is prayer? *(being with God, talking to God, listening to God)* How do you pray? . . . We each pray in different ways. Some say prayers like the "Our Father" or "Hail Mary." Some people say whatever comes to their minds. Others sit quietly listening for God or just being with God. Some like to go for walks or bike rides with God. The important thing is that we spend time both talking and listening to God. By doing this, we'll discover more about how God wants us to live.

Who Are the Raggedy Anns and Andys in Your Life?

Scripture: Mark 9:30–37
(Twenty-Fifth Sunday of the Year — B)

Preparation:

■ You will need two big dolls (I used Raggedy Ann and Andy dolls).

Homily Text:

Pretend you want to buy a big doll and the store only has Raggedy Ann and Andy dolls. You have only enough money to buy one of them. Which one will you buy? *(Ask the children to hold up their hands if they'd buy Raggedy Ann. Then ask the children who would buy Raggedy Andy to hold up their hands. The number buying each doll will probably be about equal or there will be a larger number buying Raggedy Ann. Comment on this.)*

Now let's pretend that only one Raggedy Ann and only one Raggedy Andy are left. Raggedy Ann has one leg that is peach colored *(like the rest of her skin)* instead of striped, and she looks like she fell in some dirt. Raggedy Andy looks perfectly okay. Now which one will you buy? *(Have the children raise their hands for which one they will buy. Comment on the big number that are now buying Raggedy Andy.)*

When we shop we can choose whether we want something or not. We don't have to buy something that we don't think is good enough. But it isn't the same with people. We can't ignore people or make fun of them because we think there's something wrong with them, or because they're not like us. Our gospel tells us we are to welcome and include all people. When we welcome them we are welcoming Jesus, because Jesus is within all people.

Who do you find it hard to welcome or include? *(bullies, people who are angry, handicapped people, slow learners, new people in the area . . .) (Tell a story about someone you know who has been rejected by others. Try to think of an experience that the children could relate to, perhaps from your own childhood.)*

Remember that we are called to love and accept and welcome the Raggedy Anns as well as the Raggedy Andys because in doing so we welcome God.

"You Forgot the Oatmeal in the Cookies."

Scripture: Luke 17:11–19
             (Twenty-Eighth Sunday of the Year — C)

Preparation:

■ You will need a batch of oatmeal chocolate chip cookie dough without the oatmeal in it, two spoons, and a box of oatmeal in a grocery bag.

Homily Text:

Last night I mixed up a batch of cookies but before I bake them I would like a couple of the first and second grade students to taste them and see if they are okay. *(I chose first and second grade students because they wouldn't be breaking their communion fast.)* . . . Does it taste okay? *(Yes)*

If my mom tasted this dough she would say it isn't right. In fact, she'd be able to say that by looking at it. She'd say I left out the oatmeal. *(hold up oatmeal box)* Mom thinks that if we are going to eat cookies they should be good for us so she puts oatmeal in almost all the cookies she makes. She'd say I forgot the essential ingredient.

In today's gospel, ten lepers were cured but only one returned to thank Jesus. Only one remembered the "essential ingredient" of thanks. Thanks is very important in our relationship with God. By thanking God, we're telling him that we know that he's the one who does good things for us, that he cares for us and gives us all we need.

Let's remember to include this "essential ingredient" when we pray. Let's thank God.

Sharing Our Gifts

Scripture: Matthew 25:14–30
(Thirty-Third Sunday of the Year — A)

Preparation:

■ Ask three people to help you with the skit: Brainy, Athlete, Sleepy, and Baker.

■ Make a large poster that says:

> *THINGS TO DO*
>
> -Do math assignment
> -Practice basketball free throws
> -Buy a bed
> -Bake a cake

Homily Text:

Homilist: I have a list of things to do but I need help with them. *(Hold up list of things to do and read the first item: "Do math assignment.")* I'll ask Brainy if she'll help me with my math. . . . Hey, Brainy! I need help with my math. Will you help me?

Brainy: Oh, it's easy.

Homilist: But I don't understand how you know when to add and when to subtract. It just doesn't make sense.

Brainy: I understand it. You figure it out yourself. *(Brainy walks off.)*

Homilist: *(Look at list and read "Practice basketball free throws.")* Well, maybe Athlete will help me. Athlete! Will you help me with my free throws?

Athlete: I'm busy right now. I'm practicing so I can be the best.

Homilist: It'll only take a few minutes. I just need some pointers.

Athlete: I'm just too busy.

Homilist: When will you have time?

Athlete: During Christmas break. *(Athlete turns and walks off.)*

Homilist: *(Look at list and read, "Buy a bed.")* Well, maybe Sleepy will help me pick out a bed. Sleepy! . . . Sleepy! Where are you?

Sleepy:	*(Sleepy, who has been lying down in a pew, wakes up, stretches, and sits up in the pew.)* What? What do you want?
Homilist:	Sleepy, will you help me pick out a bed?
Sleepy:	I'm too tired. I have only had twelve hours of sleep.
Homilist:	But, Sleepy, you know beds the best. After all, you have slept on more beds than anyone else.
Sleepy:	I'm just too tired. *(Sleepy lays back down.)*
Homilist:	*(Look at list.)* I have one more thing on my list. Maybe Baker will help me. Hey, Baker! Will you help me bake a cake?
Baker:	Oh, it's easy — just follow the recipe.
Homilist:	I've tried, but I just don't understand what words like "beat" and "whip" mean.
Baker:	A cookbook will tell you what they mean. I'm sure you can do it. *(Baker walks off.)*
Homilist:	*(Hold up list.)* I wanted to do one of these things today, but no one would share their gifts with me. They were like the man in today's gospel who buried his master's money instead of using it. How do you think God feels when we don't use the gifts he gave us? . . . Today let's really try to use our gifts to help the people around us.

Part Five
Being the People of God

People of God Recipe

Scripture: Colossians 3:12–14

Preparation:

■ Make two posters or handouts: Wacky Cake Recipe, People of God Recipe

---

Wacky Cake

3 cups flour
2 cups sugar   Sift
2 t. soda   Together
6 T. cocoa

Make 3 holes in the mixture; into these pour:

1. 2 t. vanilla
2. 2 T. vinegar
3. 3/4 cup vegetable oil

Pour two cups cold water over the mixture. Mix well and bake for 40 minutes at 350 degrees.

People of God

3 cups compassion
2 cups kindness   Blend
2 t. humility   Together
6 T. gentleness

Make 3 holes in the mixture; into these pour:

1. 2 t. patience
2. 2 T. helpfulness
3. 3/4 cup forgiveness

Pour two huge cups of love over the mixture. Mix well. Bake in the oven of God's love until ready to be Christ to others.

Homily Text:

How many of you have made a cake or helped make one? Today I want to show you a recipe I enjoy making. It is called a Wacky Cake because of the way it is made. *(Read through the recipe and explain how it is made.)*

Our reading today is a difficult one. Does anyone remember what it is about?... Perhaps if we think of it as a recipe it will make more sense. *(Read through the People of God recipe. Define any words the children might not know.)*

Who are the people of God? *(We are.)* How do these ingredients make us the people God wants us to be? *(do things for others, be happy and cheerful...)*

What would happen if I left the sugar out of the Wacky cake recipe? *(it wouldn't taste good)* The same is true about the People of God recipe. We need to check our lives and see that we have all the ingredients so we can be the people God calls us to be.

Linked Together

Scripture: 1 Corinthians 12:12–20, 27

Preparation:

■ Have each class make a chain out of construction paper.
Each link has the name of a child or teacher written on it.
You will need a stapler to add links to the chain.

Note:
This lesson is designed for an all-school Mass or another occasion when several smaller groups get together for one activity.

Homily Text:

What does this reading say we are? *(all one body)* A body needs all
its parts connected and working together. Another way to look at this
idea would be to use the chains you made. *(Ask two people from each
class to come to the front and hold their class chain.)*

If you look at these chains you see that each person in the class is
connected to the others; your life affects other people. We need each
other to make our chain work.

Now I'll add this link for myself. *(Connect two of the classes together; add as many more links as are needed to make the chains into
one chain. Mention people who connect the classes together, such as
the principal, the pastor, etc.)*

What if I add another link and closed the chain? Would that be
right? . . . No, because everyone is a part of the chain of God's family
— unborn babies, beggars, your parents, your family, other relatives,
people who have died, friends, enemies. . . .

What if I take this link out? Would it be right? . . . The chain
would be incomplete. We need everyone.

Today let this chain remind you that we are all important and that
everyone else in this world is important, too.

Simon Says

Scripture: John 14:21–26

Homily Text:

Who can tell me how to play "Simon Says"?... Let's play a quick game to see if you all know how to play it. *(Have the children do several things and say "Simon says" for each of them, ending with the children standing up. Now say "sit down" without saying "Simon says." This makes their mistake obvious to all. Say "Simon says, sit down.")*

What do you have to do when playing Simon Says? *(listen for the person to say "Simon says")* Then why did some of you sit down when I didn't say "Simon says"? *(not listening, got involved in the game and forgot about what they were doing, followed someone else who did it wrong...)*

In the gospel today, Jesus says we are to accept and obey his commandments and love others. Do we always do this?... Why not?... For a lot of the same reasons you didn't listen while playing Simon Says: We don't hear God, we forget the commandments, we get too busy with other things in our lives....

The last few verses of the reading tell us that Jesus gives us a gift to help us live his ways. What do you think it is? *(the Holy Spirit)* We have to listen carefully to the Holy Spirit just as we need to listen carefully when we play Simon Says.

Today let's pray for the ability to listen to the Holy Spirit so we won't be sitting when we should be standing. Let's pray that we will truly follow Jesus' way.

Discover My Gifts for You

Scripture: Mark 9:33–37

Preparation:

■ Wrap a package in gift-wrap. Bring in a self-stick package bow or a bow with masking tape attached to the back. Make a sign to hang around a child's neck that says:

To: You

From: God

■ Make a poster that says, "Discover My Gifts for You."

Homily Text:

If I were to give you this present, how many of you would take it?... Why?... If I told you I had found it on the street would you still take it?... Do you realize that it might contain something danger-ous, like a bomb?... Most of us are so curious that we would still go ahead and open it.

Our poster today says, "Discover My Gifts for You." Our church is filled with gifts. Have you found them?... Let me help you. *(Ask a student to come forward. Put the sign around his or her neck and the bow on his or her head.)*

All the people here are gifts for you. They aren't wrapped in bright paper. What are they wrapped in? *(clothes, skin, and hair)*

What would I find if I unwrapped you?... Our gospel today gives us a clue. It tells us: "Whoever welcomes a child in my name wel-comes me." So what would I find if I unwrapped you? *(Jesus)*

Today let's take the challenge to discover God's gifts to us. Let's welcome all the people in our lives as gifts.

Sack People

Scripture: Matthew 18:1–5, 10 (Guardian Angels — October 2)
              *(Note: This lesson could also be adapted for use during
              Respect Life Month — October.)*

Preparation:

■ You will need two grocery sacks. Write the name of each person in the group on small slips of paper and put them in a
   container.

Homily Text:

I need two volunteers.... I am going to put a grocery sack over
each of your heads.... *(to the rest of the children)* How many of you
have seen sack people before?... What can you tell me about sack
people? *(no hair, eyes, ears, mouth, nose...)* So, sack people can't
hear, see, smell, taste....

How many of you have treated people like sack people?... Un-
fortunately, I have. You mean none of you have ever called someone
a name? When you call someone a name, that person is hurt and
wishes he could crawl into a sack so no one could see him. How else
can you treat someone like a sack person? *(pull their hair, poke a fin-
ger in their eyes, punch their nose, yell in their ears...)*

In the gospel today, we hear Jesus say, "Never despise one of my
little ones." Never do anything that will make someone want to be a
sack person. Jesus tells us that each of us has an angel in heaven.

Jesus could have said, "Don't treat people like sack people. Instead, treat them like you are their angel, their guardian angel."
Today we celebrate guardian angels. What are they? *(they protect us,
watch over us, and, especially, pray for us)*

To help us to remember not to treat people like sack people and to
be like guardian angels, I would like you to draw the name of someone here and be especially nice to that person this week. Remember
to pray for him or her. You can help this person's guardian angel for
the week. *(Have everyone come forward to draw a name.)*

Be a Saint

Scripture: Revelation 7:2–4, 9–14 or 1 John 3:1–3
(All Saints Day)

Preparation:

■ Find one or more pictures of saints with halos. Cut the center out of a paper plate (a heavier plate works best).

Homily Text:

How many of you have ever seen someone who looks like this? *(show picture of saint with halo)* . . . What is different about this person? *(has a halo)* Right. We don't see people walking around with halos on or above their heads. Why are the halos in the pictures? *(to show us these people are holy, are saints)* Are saints people like us? . . .

Let's take this paper plate with the center cut out of it and pretend it is a halo. If we take the halo and turn it upside down, it could be a hat *(place it on a child's head)*. This can remind us that the saints are people who worked hard at what they did. What did some of the saints do? *(fed the hungry, wrote books, raised families, started religious communities, farmed, taught, nursed the sick . . .)*

The halo could also be a Frisbee *(toss it to one of the children and retrieve it)*. This reminds us that the saints weren't always serious. They had fun. Yet, we usually don't read about what they did to have fun. What do you think the saints might have done for fun? . . .

We can also use it as a halo *(place it right side up on a child's head)*. What do you think this stands for? *(the saint's relationship with God)* Saints are different from other people because they put their relationship with God before all other things, before their work and their play. They let God be a part of all of their lives.

So, when you see a picture of a saint, don't think, "They are nothing like me. I don't have a chance at being a saint." You *can* be a saint. Just remember to let God *(put halo, right side up, on your head)* be with you as you work *(put halo, upside down, on your head)* and play *(toss halo to someone and retrieve it)*.

Be Like an Octopus!
(Christian Unity Week)

Scripture: 1 Corinthians 12:12–20, 27

Preparation:

- Make an octopus out of balloons: Use a round balloon for the head and five elongated balloons for the legs (I hooked three balloons together with a rubber band. Connect the two bundles of three balloons together with another rubber band. Leave plenty of time to do this.)
- Make a poster that says, "We are all Christ's body."

Homily Text:

What is this? *(An octopus)* What does an octopus do with its legs? *(Captures shellfish for food and squeezes them to break the shells apart)* It is important for the legs to work together. Why? *(The octopus can't catch food to eat unless its legs work together. It would starve.)*

It is also important for us to work together. We are each like one of those legs. What would happen if we didn't work together? *(People would be hungry, cold, homeless,. . . .)* We are all needed.

This week we are praying for Christian unity. What do you think Christian unity is?... *(all Christians — Methodists, Lutherans, Catholics,... — working together to share Jesus' message)* Christian unity begins with us loving each other and working together.

Today our reading reminds us we are all a part of Christ's body. It reminds us to be like an octopus by loving each other and working together. We are all needed and we all need one another.

Am I to Be a Pitcher or a Pan?

Scripture: Luke 10:1–9

Preparation:

■   Bring in a pan, a pitcher, and a glass as visual aids.

Note:

I used this homily at the beginning of a three-week program on vocations.

Homily Text:

(Hold up the glass.) What is this?... What is it used for?... *(Hold up the pitcher.)* What is this?... What is it used for?... Can we use a pitcher to drink out of?... Can we use a glass to stir Kool-Aid in?...

(Hold up the pan.) What is this?... What is it used for?... Can we use a pan to stir things in?... Can we use a pan to drink out of?... But the pan was made to cook in, just like the glass was made to drink from, and the pitcher was made to pour something out of it.

The gospel today presents us with the task of figuring out what we might be called to do. The disciples were all sent out, but some taught, some preached, and some healed. Have any of you thought of what you want to be when you grow up? What? *(Call on several of the children to share their ideas.)*

Each of you can be anything you want to be when you grow up. Often people decide to be something different than what they thought when they were your age. *(Share something you thought you would do when you were little but aren't doing now.)*

The gospel calls us to keep learning about different kinds of things we might do and be. Sometimes you'll be able to help someone out by doing something that you've never thought of doing before. You might feel like a pan being used as a pitcher.

But when it's time to decide what you want to do, you will be better prepared to make that decision because of all the experiences you've had. You will be a pan being used as a pan, although you'll always be able to be a pitcher or a glass if you're needed.

Baptism

Note: This lesson could work well during the Easter season, when we renew our baptismal promises and include a sprinkling rite in the liturgy.

Preparation:

■ Have a dish of water, a branch or something to sprinkle water with, and signs that say "life," "cleansing," and "death."

■ Make a poster with water in the background; you will put the three signs on the poster with masking tape. You might also bring in pictures or mementos from a baptism (for example, a baptismal candle or gown).

Homily Text:

(Sprinkle water on the students and watch their reactions.) What did you do when I sprinkled water on you? *(wiped it off, acted surprised...)* Why?...

When you see water, what does it remind you of? *(drinks; rain; playing in water; watering animals, plants; washing; drowning...)*

Water reminds us of life: All living things need water to live. *(Add "life" sign to poster.)* Water reminds us of cleansing. We use water to wash ourselves and our things. *(Add "cleansing" sign to poster.)* Water reminds us of death: Too much water can kill living things. Have you ever watered a plant too much? People can drown in too much water, too. *(Add "death" sign to poster.)*

What sacrament uses water? *(baptism)* Why do we use water? *(reminds us that we are cleansed of original sin, that we die and rise in Christ . . .)*

Our baptismal day is very special because it is the day we are welcomed into the Christian community. *(Share a story about your own baptism or the baptism of someone you know. Show pictures or mementos. Students may also share stories of a younger brother or sister being baptized.)*

There is a holy water font by each of our church doors. Why do we dip our fingers in the water and then make the sign of the cross? *(reminds us of our baptisms)* I encourage you to go home and ask your parents about your baptism. Find out all you can about it. Then the next time you come to church and dip your fingers into the holy water, remember that very special event it recalls—your being cleansed dying, and living in the sacrament of baptism *(point to the three signs)*.

Thank You, Jesus!
(First Communion — Eucharist)

Note: This could be done at the last practice for first communion and the sign brought up during the presentation of the gifts.

Preparation:

■ Have colored pens or pencils available. Make a big thank-you card out of a folded piece of poster board so it will stand. On the front of it write, "Thank You, Jesus!"

Homily Text:

What happens this week? . . . Yes, you make your first communion. This will be the first time you come forward with the rest of the parish to receive the body and blood of Christ, to receive eucharist. What does the word *eucharist* mean? *(thanksgiving)* We come together to celebrate a prayer of thanksgiving to God, a prayer to thank God. What are we thanking God for? *(Jesus, Jesus' dying and rising, our lives with Jesus, holy communion, each other . . .)*

I invite you to write a message on this big thank-you card for Jesus or just sign your name. You children who are receiving first communion, your family and friends, and our whole parish have so much to thank God for. We are glad you are joining us at God's table.

Which Animal Are You?
(Reconciliation)

Homily Text:

How many of you have trouble thinking of sins to confess when you prepare for the sacrament of reconciliation? . . . I do. To help us to recall our sins today, let's think about whether we are like any of the following animals. *(As you mention an animal, hold up its picture. When you've finished discussing that animal, hang it on the poster.)*

- Are you busy like a bee? Are you too busy to care about and help other people?

- Are you prickly like a porcupine? Do people not want to be around you because you might stick them with words that hurt?

- Are you grouchy as a bear? Do people want to avoid you because you are often in a bad mood?
- Do you run like a deer? Do you leave the room or house or barn so you won't have to help with chores?
- Are you like a clucking chicken? Do you talk about other people behind their backs? Are you a tattle-tale? Do you ever stop talking and listen to what others are saying?
- Are you as sneaky as a snake stealing eggs? Do you steal things from others?
- Are you Snoopy? Do you get into your brothers' or sisters' or parents' things? Do you try to find out things that are none of your business?
- Are you a barking dog? Do you "bark" a lot at other people by saying things like: "I am not going to do that!"; "Get out of my way!"; "Leave me alone!"?
- Are you a pack rat? Do you "pack" things away so that others can't use them? Do you not share your things with others?

Maybe you are like an animal I haven't mentioned. Take a little time to think about which animal(s) you are like. Then ask God to forgive you and help you be a better person.

Part Six

School
Celebrations

Be Like a Cookie Monster
(Beginning of School Year)

Scripture: Psalm 119:129–135

Preparation:

■   You will need a plate of cookies, several books, and a "Be like a Cookie Monster!" book mark for each person.

Homily Text:

I have a plate of cookies. How many of you could eat all of the cookies if I let you?. . . It looks like we have a lot of cookie monsters. I have some books here, too. How many of you could read all these books?. . .

This year I challenge you to be like a cookie monster. What do cookie monsters do? *(eat cookies)* Do they eat all kinds of cookies? *(yes)* Your mind likes new information and knowledge just as much as your taste buds like the taste of cookies. How do you think you can be like cookie monsters during this school year? *(learn all you can about as many things as you can)*

Do cookie monsters ever want to stop eating cookies? *(no)* So keep learning. Don't stop. There are so many exciting things this year can hold for you. For some it may be learning to read. Others will learn to write in cursive. Others will learn how to multiply. Some of you will learn about the people in other countries. And, hopefully, each of you will learn more about yourself and about God.

I hope this year you are like a cookie monster — gaining lots of knowledge about different subjects all year long. To remind you to do this, I have "Be like a Cookie Monster" book marks for you to use this year. *(Pass out the book marks now or after Mass/class.)*

Sail, Explore, Discover
(Columbus Day)

Scripture: Genesis 12:1–4

Preparation:

- ■ Make a poster that says, "Be like Columbus."
- ■ Draw three ships on the poster with "Nina," "Pinta," and "Santa Maria" written on them. Write the words "Sail," "Explore," and "Discover" on pieces of paper.

Homily Text:

What day is today? *(Columbus Day)* What did Columbus do? *(discovered America)* We say Columbus discovered the New World, but, actually, other people had been there before him. Native Americans had lived here for hundreds of years, and some Norse explorers had landed here earlier than Columbus. Because Europeans didn't know that this "New World" existed before Columbus made his journey, they believed he discovered it.

What were the names of the ships that Columbus took on his first voyage? *(Nina, Pinta, and Santa Maria)* These ships were made of wood. They didn't have engines or motors. The crews had good compasses but they had no way to measure distance so they had to guess if they were going the right way.

Columbus had an idea that the shortest way to the Indies, where they got gold, gems, and spices, was sailing west. So Columbus sailed, explored, and discovered. He didn't find the Indies, but he did find a new continent and so much more.

In your lives you have also explored and discovered new things. You haven't discovered a new continent like Columbus did, but you learned to walk. You left the security of mom and dad's side to see what was behind the chair, under the table, in the other room . . . . You discovered the world was much bigger than you thought. What other things have you discovered? . . .

In the years ahead, you will continue to explore your world and discover new things. We never stop doing this, no matter how old we are. In our reading, we hear about God calling Abraham to leave his family and his home and journey to a new land. He did this because he trusted God to lead him. Where do you think Christopher Columbus found the strength and courage to set sail for the new world? . . . Columbus always sailed with God. He believed that God wanted him to make great discoveries so that he could spread Christianity. Columbus spent time with God at Mass and in prayer.

We need to rely on God, too, as we sail, explore, and discover. Maybe one of you will discover the cure to cancer, invent a car that runs on air, discover a cheaper way to heat and cool buildings . . . . Just remember to be like Columbus and let God sail with you. *(Place the "sail," "explore," and "discover" signs over the words, "Nina," "Pinta," and "Santa Maria" written on the ships on the poster.)*

Thanks for Our Hands
(Thanksgiving Day)

Scripture: Luke 17:11–19

Preparation:

- Cut out paper hands from different colors of construction paper.
- Make a poster that says, "God, thank you."

Homily Text:

What happened in today's gospel? *(Ten lepers were healed and only one returned to thank Jesus.)* What did Jesus ask the leper that returned? *(Why didn't the other nine lepers return to thank him, too?)*

Do you take time to thank God? . . . With Thanksgiving Day approaching we need to think about this. What are some things you are thankful for? *(Children tell different things they are thankful for.)* Are there things you forget to thank God for? . . . What about your hands? *(pass out paper hands)*

These paper hands can remind us to thank God. Write something that you're thankful for on the hand. The hands can also remind us to be thankful for the things we take for granted — our hands and feet, the fact that we're healthy, being able to breathe and dance and sing . . . .

I'd like each of us to bring forward our paper hands and tape them to the poster as a sign of our thankfulness for all that God has given us.

Jesus, You Are Our Valentine
(Valentine's Day)

Scripture: Mark 12:28b–31 or Matthew 22:34–40

Preparation:

- ■ Cover a box with red and white paper and hearts to put the valentines for Jesus in.
- ■ Make a poster that says, "Jesus, You Are Our Valentine."

Homily Text:

What day is today? *(Valentine's Day)* What do we do to celebrate Valentine's Day? *(send cards, candy, flowers)* Why do we do these things? *(to show people we care about them and love them)*

So, we send cards and gifts to those we care about and love. Who does that include? *(friends, family, classmates)* I think you left some people out. Let's look at the gospel and see who it might be. What does the gospel say? *("Love the Lord your God with all your heart, with all your soul, with all your mind, and with all your strength.")* One way we can do that is to send a valentine to Jesus. Did you think of doing that today?

What else does the gospel say? *("Love your neighbor as yourself.")* Did you send yourself a valentine? . . . Did you send your neighbors valentines? Who do you think Jesus means when he says "love your neighbor"? *(people who live next to you)* What about classmates you don't usually talk to? What about students in another class? Your neighbor can also be someone who's sick, or in a nursing home, or in prison. We are to love all these people. One way to show this love is to send a valentine. You don't have to know people to send them valentines. *(You might want to make a class project out of sending valentines to a nursing home in the area.)*

Today, I'm going to ask you to make a valentine for yourself, one for someone you usually don't give a valentine to, and one for Jesus. I'll put a box out that you can put the valentines for Jesus in. Then I'll put them on the wall with our poster.

Have a happy Valentine's Day and remember to love God, yourself, and others.

Mardi Gras

Scripture: Mark 8:22–26

Preparation:

- Decorate with balloons and crepe paper and signs that say "alleluia" to create a party atmosphere. Plan to sing songs with lots of "alleluias" in them.

Homily Text:

What day is today? *(Shrove or Fat Tuesday, Mardi Gras)* What happens on Mardi Gras? . . . What are we celebrating? *(Here is an explanation of the tradition of Mardi Gras. Use any or all of it depending on the age and interests of your students: Before there was a way to keep meat from spoiling with the occasional warm days in the spring, people would hold a party to eat all the meat that was left after the winter at one happy event. The word* carnival *was originally used for this end-of-winter holiday. Carnival means "good-bye to the meat." Once the party was over and the meat was gone, there wasn't much food to eat for several weeks, until spring. The church began to use this time of less food, a time of natural penance, for the season we call Lent. The day after the big party became a somber day when people reflected on their sins. This is what we celebrate on Ash Wednesday — our need for forgiveness and reconciliation.)*

Today is a special day. We celebrate. We sing "Alleluia." What does *alleluia* mean? *(praise Yahweh, praise the Lord)* Today we sing lots of alleluias because we won't sing it again until Easter. The church doesn't sing alleluia during Lent. Instead we focus on our need for God's mercy and love. Lent will prepare us to sing alleluia with all our hearts on Easter.

What happened in today's gospel? *(a blind man was healed)* Was he healed all at once? *(no)* It was a gradual healing. The same is true for us. We gradually open up to God. Each year during Lent we have another opportunity to be a little more open to Christ.

Tomorrow we begin Lent. The party will be over for six weeks of fasting and prayer and giving money to the poor. But today we celebrate and enjoy the life and gifts God has given us.

Flavors of Faith
(Closing of the School Year)

Preparation:

- ■ Make blank ice cream cones out of brown construction paper and add paper "scoops" of different colored ice cream.
- ■ Make a paper ice cream cone for each child; write on it: "What flavor is my faith today?"
- ■ You will need tape and a marker.
- ■ Make a poster that says, "Flavors of Faith."

Homily Text:

How many of you like to eat ice cream during the summer? What are some of your favorite flavors? . . . Just as there are many different flavors of ice cream, there are also many different flavors or parts to our faith. Let's see if you can name some of them. What did you learn about God and your faith this year? . . . *(As the children name things, write each idea on an ice cream cone and tape it to the poster.)*

This summer you won't be spending as much time studying about God and faith. But you will be living your faith every day. And every day you live with God by your side. To remind you to practice what you've learned this year, I've made an ice cream cone for each of you to take home. It says, "What flavor is my faith today?" Put it someplace where you will see it and ask yourself each day, "What part of God or my faith did I experience today?"

By the time you return to school next year, I bet you will have eaten many different flavors of ice cream. And I pray that you will also have lived many different "flavors" of your faith.

Index of Scripture Readings

Luke 1:26b–35, 38
Jesus Is the Light in Our Lives (Fourth Sunday of Advent — B)

Luke 1:39–45
Trust Like Mary (Fourth Sunday of Advent — C)

Luke 5:1–11
Jesus' Net (Fifth Sunday of the Year — C)

Luke 9:18–24
Be a Butterfly (Twelfth Sunday of the Year — C)

Luke 10:1–9
Am I to Be a Pitcher or a Pan? (Vocations)

Luke 11:1–13
Taking Time for God (Seventeenth Sunday of the Year — C)

Luke 15:11–24
I Lost My . . . (Fourth Sunday of Lent — C)

Luke 17:11–19
"You Forgot the Oatmeal in the Cookies."
   (Twenty-Eighth Sunday of the Year — C)
Thanks for Our Hands (Thanksgiving Day)

Luke 24:13–35
Follow the Yellow Brick Road (Third Sunday of Easter — A)

John 6:1–15
Let's Be Like Honeybees (Seventeenth Sunday of the Year — B)

John 10:11–16
Which Shepherd Do You Follow? (Fourth Sunday of Easter — B)

John 14:1–12
Are You Following Your Compass? (Fifth Sunday of Easter — A)

John 14:21–26
Simon Says

John 20:19–23
"Piece" Be With You
   (Second Sunday of Easter — A, B, or C [partial])

Acts 1:1–11
Up, Up, and Away (Ascension)

Acts 2:1–13
Happy Birthday to Us! (Pentecost)
The Holy Spirit (Pentecost)

1 Corinthians 1:3–9
Gifts From Jesus (First Sunday of Advent — B)

1 Corinthians 12:12–20, 27
Linked Together
Be Like an Octopus! (Christian Unity Week)

2 Corinthians 5:20 — 6:2
Which Body Are You? (Ash Wednesday)

Galatians 2:19b–20
The Lenten Snake

Ephesians 6:18b–19
Pray Always

Colossians 3:12–14
People of God Recipe

1 Thessalonians 3:12 — 4:2
Add Vent (First Sunday of Advent — C)

1 Thessalonians 5:16–24
Have You Checked Your "Oil" Lately? (Third Sunday of Advent — B)

1 John 3:1–3
Be a Saint (All Saints Day)

1 John 4:7–10
Mirror, Mirror (Sixth Sunday of Easter — B)

1 John 4:11–16
Mirror, Mirror (Seventh Sunday of Easter — B)

1 John 5:1–6
Mirror, Mirror (Second Sunday of Easter — B)

Revelation 7:2–4, 9–14
Be a Saint (All Saints Day)